Anonymous

An Enquiry Into the Conduct of a Late Right Honourable

Commoner

Anonymous

An Enquiry Into the Conduct of a Late Right Honourable Commoner

ISBN/EAN: 9783337195762

Printed in Europe, USA, Canada, Australia, Japan

Cover: Foto ©Suzi / pixelio.de

More available books at **www.hansebooks.com**

AN ENQVIRY INTO THE CONDVCT OF A LATE RIGHT HONOVRABLE COMMONER.

" Plain Truth, Dear Pynſent, needs no Flow'rs
" of Speech."

POPE.

LONDON: Printed for J. ALMON, oppo-
poſite Burlington-Houſe, in Piccadilly.

Speedily will be publifhed,

An EXAMINATION of the Principles, and boafted Disinterestedness, of a Late RIGHT HONOURABLE Gentleman. With a *Poft-fcript* concerning his Friends.

Quem maxumè odifti, ei maxumè obfequeris: aliud ftans, aliud fedens, de Republica fentis: his maledicis, illos odifti, leviffume transfuga: neque in hâc, neque in illâ parte fidem habes.

SALLUST.

Printed for J. Almon, oppofite Burlington-House, Piccadilly.

AN ENQVIRY INTO THE CONDVCT OF A LATE RIGHT HONOVRABLE COMMONER.

IN the tide of almoſt every great man's life, there is commonly one period, which is not only more remarkable than the reſt, but conveys with it ſtrong characteriſtic marks of the complexion of him to whom it belongs. Thus the great BACON, when he ſaw the only road to preferment was thro' BUCKINGHAM, attached himſelf to that Favourite, and undertook to ſecond the views of the crown : we read of his exceſſive pliancy in tranſactions wholly below his rank and character ; particularly ſeveral attempts to corrupt and bias the

B   judges,

judges, in caufes which the King or his minifter had much at heart. " Ava- " rice," fays Mr. Juftice Fos T E R, (who in his difcourfe on high treafon has re- corded thefe inftances of his bafenefs) " I think was not his ruling paffion. " But whenever a falfe ambition, ever " reftlefs and craving, over-heated in " the purfuit of the honours which " the crown alone can confer, hap- " peneth to ftimulate an heart other- " wife formed for great and noble " purfuits, it hath frequently betray- " ed it into meafures full as mean as " avarice itfelf could have fuggefted to " the wretched animals, who live and " die under her dominion. For thefe " paffions, however they may feem to " be at variance, have ordinarily pro- " duced the fame effects. Both de- " grade the man ; both contract his " views

" views into the little point of felf-in-
" tereft, and equally fteel the heart
" againft the rebukes of confcience,
" or the fenfe of true honour." Who-
ever is at the pains of reading BA-
CON's life, will find, that from the
moment of his attaching himfelf to
VILLIERS, duke of BUCKINGHAM, his
character takes a new turn. We fee
no more of the firm friend, nor
honeft man : both are funk in the
fcandalous Inftrument of a Favourite,
without honour ; and a court, without
veracity. And VILLIERS, and he, were
afterwards impeached by the Commons. The King indeed endeavoured
to fave VILLIERS; but BACON was facrificed. It is true, he had been made a
lord, but he was fequeftered from parliament ; and the pangs of his confcience, and the warmth of his regrets,

were

were evidenced by every paſſage of his future life.

Within our own times, who had a more exalted character, or whoſe popularity was higher, than Mr. WILLIAM PULTENEY'S ? He was the *Great Commoner* of his time; the terror of corruption, the ſupport of virtue; the firm, diſintereſted patriot. But when he, treacherouſly, deſerted his friends, meanly capitulated with the court, bargained ſtill more abjectly to ſcreen the Favourite, and accepted of a peerage, his popularity forſook him in an inſtant: the united public looked upon him as a traitor, and were unanimous in condemning, deteſting, and execrating him. His quondam friends abhorred him, and his enemies deſpiſed him. That one tranſaction hath branded his name with eternal infamy.

Other

Other inftances of the like nature
are not wanting; but thefe are enough
to eftablifh this great truth, that men
who are innately bad, notwithftanding
the force of a long habit of hypocrify,
will, one time or other, wear their natural complexion.

This is the criterion of a LATE.
Right Honourable COMMONER, juft
called to another houfe. He has long
dwelt as high in the public efteem, as
Mr. PULTENEY once did, confidered
to have talents fuperior to BACON,
and fuppofed to have more integrity than either. The people have ado-
red him to a degree more zealous, than
perhaps any other man ever experien-
ced; and upon repeated and pofitive affurances of his difintereftednefs, they
have been led to repofe in him the
moft unlimited confidence. However,

ever, there have not been wanting
many who have fufpected the veracity
of thofe affurances; and, whofe penetration being guided by a true know-
ledge of fome parts of his conduct,
have frequently afferted, he would
one day or other prove *an Impoftor*.

A fketch of fome parts of his former
conduct will not be amifs in this
place, as it will remind the public,
what hair-breadth efcapes he has had
of lofing his popularity, and will
in fome meafure be found to lead
to the caufes of his laft great manœvre;
the grand criterion by which the public
opinion of his boafted fidelity and patriotifm, will be for ever fixed upon
the folid foundation of indifputable
Truth.

None was more forward or more
violent, in declaiming with virulence
againft

against Sir ROBERT WALPOLE. By this he first became popular; and the Dutchefs of MARLBOROUGH left him ten thoufand pounds, with the intention of preferving him *unplaced* and *unpenfioned.* Next he condemned the PELHAMS, and their adminiftration, to the fhades of Erebus, as the moft pernicious men, and moft deftructive meafures ever known and adopted. They knew his price, and he entered into a compromife with the Duke of NEWCASTLE, who made him a Vice-Treafurer of IRELAND, with the late Lord CHOLMONDELEY. He then poured the moft lavifh encomiums upon them, and deified Sir ROBERT WALPOLE. For the truth of thefe facts, I appeal to the great number of perfons now alive who are well acquainted with them; and to fome, who have copies of a few of

the

the moſt remarkable paſſages in his ſtrange, inconſiſtent, and contradictory ſpeeches. By this conduct his popularity was well nigh being ruined, but his friends and relations were indefatigable in ſupporting his character; and he himſelf neglected neither pains nor opportunity of acquiring an intereſt at St. James's, by paying court to a Female Favourite, who at that time held the keys of promotion. And by an intereſt as ſcandalous, as his conduct was obſequious, he obtained the poſt of Paymaſter. For a little time he was quiet, but his ever reſtleſs ambition, ſoon broke out, and he aimed at the ſole guidance of the State, which he ſeemed reſolved to take by ſtorm. He thundered againſt HANOVER, the very name of which he was for expunging out of the dictionary; it was called a

mill-

mill-ftone hung about the neck of Great-Britain, and ftiled the bane of this country, from the expence which it coft us; and the moft folemn declarations were made, that not a fhilling nor a man fhould go to Germany. The popular gale wafts him into power: and though not to that degree of eminence in ftation, which conftitutionally gives the lead in public bufinefs, yet he ufurped an abfolute dominion over the whole court. It is his nature to bear no controul, therefore the King was taken captive in his clofet, and made prifoner upon his throne. But as it were to atone for this conduct, and to give the public another proof, that not theirs, but his own intereft, was the object he had in view; though abfolute minifter, and of courfe at full liberty to

C

carry

carry on the war upon whatever fyftem he pleafed, and a neutrality fe-
cured for Hanover; yet he entered
into all the predelictions of his Sove-
reign, broke the neutrality in Germany, and notwithftanding his many
furious and energetic declarations a-
gainft the continent, the very founds
of which were tingling in our ears, he
plunged us deeper into the German
war than any of his predeceffors; fent
over more men and more money than
any other minifter ever dared; and at
an expence of above eighty millions,
conquered America in Germany. *

And

* It is only curious, from obfervation of his
natural inconfiftency, to mention, that when
the late lord Anfon was attacked in the Houfe
of Commons upon the lofs of Minorca, the
Late Commoner (knowing that the late Lord
Hardwicke was then the Court Favourite) ftood
up to vindicate his Lordfhip, and faid, " that
" he

And to fupport this enormous load
of expence, it was at his exprefs in-
junction, that the laft heavy additional
duty was laid upon beer, even in oppofition to the Duke of NEWCASTLE
and the late Mr. LEGGE, who would
otherwife have laid a tax upon the lux-
uries of life, in order to fpare the in-
duftrious, and put the burden upon the
rich and idle. As it falls almoft exclufively upon the moft ufeful and labori-
ous part of the nation, it may with
ftrict juftice be ftiled a grievous and
an oppreffive tax, by which the price
of one article of confumption was ad-
vanced a *Seventh.*———A tax cruelly

wrung

" he was convinced his Lordfhip had erred
" through want of intellect, and not through
" defign." After this extraordinary declaration, he reftored his Lordfhip to that very
poft, for which he had pronounced him unqua-
lified through deficiency of underftanding.

wrung from the briny fweat of induf-
try, and which feems to have been
founded on no other principle, than
that in order to render the people de-
pendent, we fhould begin by making
them poor.

Ever wifhing to attain and preferve
power by any facrifice or any means,
and finding foon after the acceffion
of his prefent Majefty, that the Earl
of BUTE was in poffeffion of the r—
ear, he was the firft and principal inftrument of that noble Lord's introduction to power; particularly to
the poft of Secretary of State and coadjutor to himfelf; which fhews, as
clearly as any thing can, his early and
clofe connexion with the Favourite.
And upon what principle could this
be done, but the hope of thereby lay-
ing

ing the foundation of fecurity to himfelf ?

When the Favourite had gained the
afcendancy, and had formed defigns
incompatible with the honour of the
crown and the intereft of the kingdom; when he had drawn the fub-
ftance and the fhadow likewife of
ftrength from the Great Commoner,
and defeated him alfo in his mighty
defign upon Spain; then, even then,
notwithftanding this infult, and many
others, fuch was either his luft for
office, or his friendfhip for the Favourite, that he would have facrificed
his haughty overbearing fpirit to a
fufferance of remaining in office, and
fubmitted to a controul not only contradictory of all his former principles, but infamous in the eyes of the
public : had it not been for the fpirited

rited and truly patriotic refentment of his moft noble friend and relation, Earl TEMPLE; who with a magnanimity, almoft peculiar to himfelf, difdained to wear the chains, or put on the livery of fuch an incompetent Statefman, fuch a contemptible being; and firft ftrongly urged, and at length FORCED the COMMONER into *refignation*; which he accompanied with his own, in order to give an example of fpirit and refiftance to an *Ufurpation*, fo exceedingly dangerous to both court and people.

Notwithftanding the moft virulent and unjuftifiable profcription carried on againft the Late Commoner, and his friends, by the influence of the Favourite; notwithftanding the introduction of men by the fame power who had long been hateful to him;

not-

notwithſtanding a total alteration of meaſures ; and notwithſtanding the moſt iniquitous ſacrifices made of the Honour, and Faith of the Crown, and of the Glory and Intereſt of the People ; yet did he on that day, that important day, when the permanency of England was under conſideration, ſhrink back ; and cover his boaſted patriotiſm in a three hours ſpeech *upon equilibrium.* He was for and againſt the preliminaries of peace ; he liked and he diſliked them ; and in a word, he was full of nothing but doubts and hopes and fears. If he really did not approve of them, and in his own heart he could not do otherwiſe, why did he not declare his ſentiments boldly like a true patriot ? The reaſon is, he knew the peace to be the favourite meaſure of the Minion, and he was afraid

fraid of doing him too much mifchief
on that occafion ; apprehending that a
fpirited and nervous oppofition on that
queftion, might lay the foundation of
an irreparable breach ; might deftroy
for ever his purpofe, which was already formed, of obtaining a reconcilia-
tion with the Earl of BUTE.*

And

* " It is more than probable, he knew his
channel of conveyance to Mr. Pitt ; and that
a communication had, for fome time, been
opened between them, elfe what reafon can be
given for Mr. Beckford's conduct, who was
Lord Mayor of London at the time of making the peace, in not calling a Court of Common Council, to prepare and prefent petitions
to Parliament againft the Preliminary Articles.
This behaviour would have been fpirited, and
worthy the metropolis of England, which fo
zealoufly condemned thofe articles, and the
treaty itfelf. If that ftep had been taken, it is
not very probable the vote of approbation
would have been fo much to the Favourite's
Honour." *History of Minority*, pag. 215.

And fo firmly perfuaded was the Favourite of the Great Commoner's wifhes to accomplifh fuch an union, that he foon afterwards employed Sir HARRY ERSKINE to open a negocia- tion for that purpofe. There are not wanting thofe who know of Sir HARRY's going from place to place, and from man to man, in fearch of a channel to convey the Favourite's de- figns, in a *proper manner* (as it was phrafed) to Mr. BECKFORD, who was Mr. PITT's great and confidential friend. As foon as the plan was known, it was accepted. And Lord BUTE went in difguife in the middle of the night, in Auguft 1763, to Mr. PITT's own houfe in Jermyn-ftreet. And it is as certain, that the Great Commoner, in his fubfequent confe- rences with a Greater Perfonage, to whom the door was opened for him

D

by

by the Minion, *would have accepted, and united with the Favourite,* had he not been preferved by the ftrong efforts of his friends.

As a proof how much the mifcarriage of this negotiation, and of courfe this intended connection with the Favourite, was againft the Commoner's wifhes, let us only recollect the extraordinary language of his friends upon that occafion; I mean of thofe few who were exclufively attached to him. " It were foolifh, faid one of them, " if a womanifh *idea of confiftency*, that " is, of acting always with the *fame* " man, fhould influence Mr. PITT to " go wrong. The great and noble " confiftency of a patriot is *fteadily* " [fine bombaft!] to purfue his coun- " try's good, and whether in the " changes of time a NEWCASTLE, " a GERMAN WHORE, or a lord " BUTE,

" Bute, may be the inftrument, it
" matters little to his country." Here
is a clear avowal of the wifh to come
into office with fuch a connexion:
And I appeal to the members of the
lower houfe, for what he himfelf has
faid there upon the fubject of a connection with the Favourite. Did he
ever fay that he had any objections
to it ? On the contrary has he not repeatedly declared, that he had none ?
and that the Favourite might, if he
pleafed, lead him into the clofet ?
This is fpeaking pretty plainly, fo
plain that it needs no comment. There
is one circumftance more ; a particular friend of his at that time, faid,
" That an *union* between Mr. PITT
" and Lord BUTE was the *only* thing
" that could give us our juft weight
" and importance abroad, and reftore
" peace and harmony at home." And

D 2   this

this friend was known to be a retailer of the Late Commoner's fentiments. From thefe particulars, and the manner in which the negotiation was fet on foot, it appears, beyond a doubt, that the Great Commoner wifhed for fuch a junction; and that he was as ready to pay court to the reigning Favourite, as ever he had been to the Countefs of Y—m—th, but was obftructed by the means of his friends.

How did the Great Commoner be-have after this? Did he not join the Favourite's party in their purfuit of an unfortunate exile?———Did he not previoufly declare in the lobby to one of the Surry members, that that un-fortunate perfon muft be fupported? But a few hours afterwards was he not the firft to put a poniard in his heart, (with his ufual diffimulation and affected piety) at the mention of
a poem,

a poem, which he had feen and read before? Did he not with a bitternefs of expreffion that could be dictated by nothing but his zeal of foliciting the Favourite's efteem, condemn and tra- duce that unhappy man? Did he not emphatically call him, " The blaf- " phemer of his God, and the libeller " of his King?" and this before any judgment could be had, although the neceffary procefs was going forward, in the courts below? It was a cenfure and condemnation which the Favou- rite had much at heart, and the affif- tance of the Great Commoner was doubtlefs very acceptable; and very probably, as it was intended, there is no doubt but it was favourably report- ed elfewhere.

In the courfe of the fame feafon, we faw him firft efpoufe, and then fly from

the

the great caufe of Public Liberty,
which his Honourable Relation had
been indefatigable in his attempts, and
had expended immenfe fums, to bring
to a determination. It is true, he affifted in the firft debate upon general
warrants; but finding that fome of
the party were in earneft in their defigns of going further, and had pre-
pared a motion againft the feizure of
papers, which was in fact the great
grievance *; and alfo finding, that the

Favourite

* They were afraid of attempting any thing
further, left they fhould thereby ruin the proba-
bility of their fuppofed fuccefs: Which was
the reafon of their not making a fecond effort,
upon a motion they had formed againft the feizure of papers, which was generally expected.
That was a point of real importance to the Liberty of the fubject ; and a condemnation of a
practice fo horrid and illegal as the feizure of
Papers undoubtedly was, would have given the
moft fenfible pleafure to every Englifhman.

But

Favourite dreaded the Minority gaining a victory, left the party fhould be
afterwards turned againft him; and
that the Favourite had therefore fupported

But the real truth is, thefe patriots by halves
only, when they were in office, were as
ftrong prerogative men as thofe whom they
now oppofed; and hoping fhortly to be in
office again, they did not chufe to condemn a
practice, which many of them held to be both
juftifiable and neceffary. So that this minority
were not fuch warm and fincere friends to Liberty as they pretended: Though they were at
infinite pains, and fome expence, to make the
public believe their profeffions, from their at-
tempt to condemn General Warrants. But
not a ftep would they take towards either re-
medying or condemning the greater grievance,
relative to papers; not an inch further would
they go although they were fure of carrying
the queftion. If it be legal to feize papers
(and fuch filence almoft implies it) it is a matter of indifference to the unfortunate perfon
whofe houfe is plundered for them, whether
the fearch and feizure are made under the authority of a general or a particular warrant;

if

ported the adminiftration with all his might upon this occafion; the Great Patriot fcandaloufly *withdrew from the caufe and the party*; and there-

by

if a general warrant will not do, a particular one may foon be had : a Secretary of State can never be many minutes in finding a Juftice of Peace to iffue a warrant for him. The queftion is, Is fuch a practice legal ? The Minority would not fay, *No.* Many of them are fuppofed to approve of it, in certain cafes ; as in high treafon, &c. but they would neither tell the public what thefe cafes were, nor under what reftrictions the practice ought to be put. They hung out a fpecious, but deceitful, appearance of Liberty, a kind of *a will with a wifp*, and intreated the public to follow it. — The evafion of the Habeas Corpus, and the clofe imprifonment, were wholly indefenfible, and would have afforded them moft excellent queftions. Thofe tranfactions were clearly againft law, and therefore ought to have been cenfured. Perhaps with refpect to the warrant, the right and beft way of proceeding would have been to have moved a complaint againft the Secretary himfelf; at

leaft

by *preventing* any point being then gained towards that fecurity of Public Liberty, which the whole kingdom fo ardently wifhed for, and expected.

A fhort time afterwards, when an impeachment of the Favourite was privately rumoured among a few only; and it was faid, that there was ftrong evidence ready to be given, particularly with regard to the peace; when a certain baronet, and others, who took fome pains in order to come at this evidence, and the conditions upon which it might have been obtained were trifling (not pecuniary) and who thought it neceffary, that the Great Commoner fhould be confulted

E

upon

leaft it would have been the moft conftitutional, and moft becoming the dignity of Parliament. But the Minority did not aim at doing juftice to the laws of their country. The bent of their defires was to get into office." *Minority, pag.* 283.

upon a subject of such importance, especially too as he was looked upon to be the fittest person to lead, or principally support such a procedure; and when, in consequence of that idea, he was applied to by one of his own friends, and in some measure a distant relation, he checked the whole in the bud, by declaring vehemently against it.

In the succeeding year (1765) the Favourite and the administration being at variance, the Great Commoner kept aloof. He wished to see them destroyed, from his personal animosity to some of them; and he did not therefore interrupt the Minion in any of his favourite measures, neither on the question of the Regency, nor any other; but waited for the opportunity, or rather the necessity, which he thought

thought the diſtreſs of the Public ſer-
vice, and the impoſſibility of carrying
on the Public buſineſs, in ſuch a
ſcene of continual warfare between
the court and the miniſtry, would in-
diſpenſibly produce, of calling him to
the ſtate : not merely as one *leſs hoſtile*
againſt the Favourite than any other
perſon, but becauſe there then was,
and had been for ſome time, a good
underſtanding between them. A negotiation was accordingly opened ;
and it was apparently with the deſign,
and expectation, of getting certain
great and favourite conditions compli-
ed with, that ſuch pains were taken to
prevail upon a ROYAL PERSONAGE
(now no more) to become the negotiator. But unfortunately for this
ſcheme, they began with the wrong
man. His ROYAL HIGHNESS firſt

ſent

sent for Lord Temple. That noble
Lord refused the conditions with a
firmness that does honour to his integrity. He then knew nothing of
what Mr. Pitt would do. His
Royal Highness went to Mr.
Pitt; and offered him the same
conditions which had been refused by
the noble Lord. And why the Great
Commoner did not chuse to accept of
them, cannot be accounted for, unless
it was because he thought them too
hard; and apparently favouring so
much of the *Butean* system, that he
was afraid to desert his noble relation,
who obviously stood upon such a
public ground; and besides, having no
subterfuge to cover the deceit and
treachery of so scandalous a connection, as that with the Favourite, must,
and would have been considered.

In

In the fucceeding negotiation (which was but a few weeks after) he was again faved by his noble Relation, who a fecond time declared his refufal to enlift under the banner of the Favourite. Again was the great Commoner foiled; and he was ftill afraid to break with his noble friend upon fuch a declaration ; but it is impoffible to exprefs the chagrin he felt in not being able to accomplifh his project, which was nothing more than the very title and place he now enjoys; the one to be obtained by the favour, and the other to be held under the tenure of the Earl of BUTE. From both of which he was prevented, and his character preferved another year, by the fuperior virtue, firmnefs, and true patriotifm of the Earl TEMPLE, who repeatedly declared, with an emphafis

phafis of zeal that fhews him to be the real friend of his country, and acting wholly upon public-fpirited principles, that he would never fubmit to a *Butal* and *Ducal* adminiftration. And in return for this fincere friendfhip, and moft effential fervice, the Commoner moft vehemently enveighed againft the noble Lord for his *obftinacy*, as he phrafed it. And he repeatedly faid to every gentleman who vifited him in the weft laft year, that he knew of no reafons which could or ought to have prevented Lord TEMPLE's acceptance. A plain and convincing proof this, that he himfelf had no objections to leaguing with the Favourite upon any terms, even tho' they were, that Lord NORTHUMBERLAND fhould be Lord Chamberlain, Mr. STUART MACKENZIE (Lord

BUTE's

Bute's brother) Privy Seal for Scotland; and that all the Favourite's friends fhould remain; nor to feeing the whole minifterial fyftem thus contaminated with the power, intereft, and influence of the Favourite. And, above all, let his lady, let his own fervants declare, if they dare, the rage he was in, the madnefs with which he was afflicted, and the intolerable uneafinefs of mind which were vifible in his fpeech and conduct for a confiderable time afterwards, occafioned by his difappointment of not going into office, with the intention, and fettled condition, of accepting in a few weeks after the firft arrangements had taken place, the very Peerage and the office of Privy Seal he hath now taken. And nothing could equal the vexation he fuffered by his own timidity, in not

deferting

deferting his noble friend and relation
at that time, and for the very purpofe
above-mentioned. But to open a
door for his future advancement, he
took the advantage of the weaknefs of
the adminiftration at the beginning of
laft winter, when there was a diverfity
of opinions amongft them concerning
the American Stamp Act, to offer them
his affiftance ; taking for granted, I
fhould imagine, that they in return
would gratify him with whatever place
and title he defired, and would be glad
of obtaining, *upon any terms*, fuch an
acceffion to their party; and when
the moft difficult bufinefs had been got
over, he wanted to change that adminiftration, part of whom it is known
he advifed to accept. Finding, however, that he could not accomplifh his
views that way, owing to the firmnefs
which

which the cabinet of that adminiftration made to a principle fo abominable
and felfifh, he turned againft them before the end of the feffion.

WE come now to this laft *Negotia-*
tion ; the grand criterion by which
the difinterefted, honeft public will
judge of the Great Commoner's character, affifted in fome meafure, as
they doubtlefs will, by the feveral irre-
futable facts already related; many
of which naturally lead, and tend to
an explanation of the caufes of this
Great, and to the world, unexpected
event. A *Negotiation* inftituted by
the Favourite, and carried on by the
noble Lawyer lately removed from
his own department to another high
office in the ftate, and haftened, too,
by embracing of the firft opportunity
to fcatter the feeds of difcord in the

F   cabinet,

cabinet, and from thence to pro-
nounce the incapacity and weaknefs
of the fuppofed Minifters. The error
laft year had been in confulting Lord
TEMPLE *firſt*. This year another
method was taken, Mr. PITT was
firſt applied to; and after that gentleman had had a conference firft with
the late Lord Chancellor, and then
with His M. Lord TEMPLE was fent
for, who directly after his coming to
town, waited on His M. at Richmond. Next day (July 16, 1766) his
Lordfhip received a very affectionate
letter from Mr. PITT, then at North-
End, Hampftead, defiring to fee his
Lordfhip there, as his health would
not permit him to come to town. His
Lordfhip went, and Mr. PITT acquainted him, that His M. had been
gracioufly pleafed to fend for h im to
form

form an adminiſtration; and as he
thought his Lordſhip "*indiſpenſable*,"
he deſired His M. to ſend for him,
and to put him at the head of the
Treaſury; and that he himſelf would
take the poſt of Privy Seal. The
Commoner then produced a liſt of
ſeveral perſons, which he ſaid *he* had
fixed upon to go in with his Lordſhip; and which he added was not to
be altered. Lord TEMPLE ſaid, that
he had had the honour of a conference
with His M. at Richmond the evening
before, and that he did not under-
ſtand from what paſſed between them,
that Mr. PITT was to be *abſolute
Maſter*, and to form *every part* of the
adminiſtration; if he had, he would
not have given himſelf the trouble of
coming to Mr. PITT upon that ſub-
ject, being determined to come in

upon

upon an *equality* with Mr. PITT, in
cafe he was to occupy the moft refponfible place under the government.
And as Mr. PITT had chofen only a
Side-Place, without any refponfibility
annexed to it, he fhould infift upon
fome of his friends being in the Cabinet Offices with him, and in whom
he could confide; which he thought
Mr. PITT could have no objection
to, as he muft be fenfible he could
not come in with honour, unlefs he
had fuch nomination; nor did he de-
fire, but that Mr. PITT fhould have
his fhare of the nomination of *his*
friends. And his Lordfhip added, that
he made a *facrifice* of his brother
Mr. GEORGE GRENVILLE, who
notwithftanding his being entirely
out of place, and excluded from all
connection with the intended fyftem,
would

would neverthelefs, fupport the meafures of their adminiftration : that it was his idea to conciliate all parties, which was the ground that had made Mr. PITT's former adminiftration fo refpectable and glorious, and to form upon the folid bafis of *Union*, an able and refponfible adminiftration, to brace the relaxed finews of government, retrieve the honour of the crown, and purfue the permanent intereft of the Public. But that if Mr. PITT infifted upon a fuperior dictation, and did not chufe to join in a plan defigned for the reftoration of that *Union*, which at no time was ever fo neceffary, he defired the conference might be broke off, and that Mr. PITT would give himfelf no further trouble about him, for that he would not fubmit to the propofed conditions.

Mr.

Mr. PITT, however, infifted upon continuing the conference; and afked, who thofe perfons were whom his Lordfhip intended for fome of the cabinet employments? His Lordfhip anfwered, that one in particular, was a noble Lord of approved character, and known abilities, who had laft year refufed the very office now offered to him [Lord TEMPLE] though preffed to it in the ftrongeft manner, by the Duke of CUMBERLAND, and the Duke of NEWCASTLE; and who being their common friend, he did not doubt Mr. PITT himfelf had in contemplation. This worthy and refpectable perfon was Lord LYTTELTON. At the conclufion of this fentence, Mr. PITT faid, Good God, how can you compare him to the Duke of GRAFTON, Lord SHELBURNE, and Mr.

Mr. CONWAY? Befides, faid he, *I* have taken the privy feal, and he cannot have that. Lord TEMPLE then mentioned the poft of Lord Prefident : upon which Mr. PITT faid, that could not be, for he had engaged the precedency : but, fays he, Lord LYTTELTON *may have a penfion.* To which Lord TEMPLE immediately anfwered, that would never do; nor would he ftain the bud of his adminiftration with an accumulation of penfions. It is true, Mr. PITT vouchfafed to permit the noble Lord to nominate his own board; but at the fame time infifted, that if two perfons of that board, (THOMAS TOWNSHEND, and GEORGE ONSLOW, Efqrs;) were turned out, they fhould have a compenfation, i. e. *Penfions.*

Mr.

Mr. PITT next aſked, what perſon his Lordſhip had in his thoughts for Secretary of State? His Lordſhip anſwered, Lord GOWER, a man of great abilities, and whom he knew to be equal to any Mr. PITT had named, and of much greater alliance; and in whom he meant and hoped to unite and conciliate a great and powerful party, in order to widen and ſtrengthen the bottom of his adminiſtration, and to vacate even the idea of oppoſition; thereby to reſtore unanimity in parliament, and confine every good man's attention to the real objeéts of his country's welfare. And his Lordſhip added, that he had never imparted his deſign to Lord GOWER, nor did he know whether that noble Lord would accept of it *, but mentioned it

---

* Lord Temple afterwards wrote to Lord Gower, to excuſe the mention he had made of his name.

it now, only as a comprehenſive meaſure, to attain the great end he wiſh-
ed, of reſtoring unanimity by a re-
conciliation of parties, that the buſineſs of the nation might go on without interruption, and become the only buſineſs of parliament. But Mr.
PITT rejected this propoſal, evident-
ly *healing* as it appeared, by ſaying,
that he had determined Mr. CONWAY
ſhould ſtay in his preſent office, and
that he had Lord SHELBURNE to pro-
poſe for the other office, then held by
the Duke of RICHMOND; ſo that
there remained no room for Lord
GOWER. This Lord TEMPLE ſaid,
was coming to his firſt propoſition of
being ſole and abſolute dictator, to
which no conſideration ſhould ever induce him to ſubmit. And therefore
he inſiſted upon ending the conference;

G   which

which he did with saying, That if he
had been firſt called upon by the K.
he ſhould have conſulted Mr. PITT's
honour, with regard to the arrangements of miniſters, and have given
him an equal ſhare in the nomination;
and that he thought himſelf ill-treat-
ed by Mr. PITT, in his not obſerving
the like conduct.

Had Mr. PITT not choſen to refuſe
a plan of government, ſo obviouſly
calculated and deſigned for the good
of the country, and for putting an
end to thoſe unhappy diviſions which
have long obſtructed the Public buſineſs, we ſhould have ſeen an adminiſtration formed of the moſt able and
upright men in the kingdom; acting
upon principles agreeable to the Public wiſhes; and whoſe natural ſtrength
and alliances, would have given ſuch

a ſtaa ſtability to their power, as would have afforded the moſt ſincere ſatiſfaction to the Public; who are concerned and grieved at theſe repeated *changes*, made apparently without any deſign of reſtoring peace to the kingdom, or any deſire of putting the direction of affairs into capable hands : *Changes* obviouſly patched up, and conſiſting of nothing but a temporary ſucceſſion of men, whoſe names were almoſt unknown till they appeared in the Gazette : *Changes* made by the Favourite, and deſigned to render all ſets of men contemptible, that he may at length, like Cardinal MAZARINE, publicly reſume his power, and tell the people he is the only capable man in the kingdom.

G 2 A French

A French Hiſtorian * has given us
the character of that Favourite French
miniſter in theſe words ;

" His perſon was handſome, his
" manners polite, and his diſcourſe in-
" ſinuating. The Queen-mother was
" extremely charmed with him, and
" he became the ſoul of all her coun-
" cils. He was almoſt impenetrable
" in his deſigns, diſguiſed in his pro-
" ceedings, artful in his intrigues, and
" often attained his ends by ſuch
" ways as would ſeem to carry him
" wide of his mark." And VOL-
TAIRE ſays, (in his Siecle de Louis
XIV. for it was during the minority
of that Prince, that this man flouriſh-
ed) " That the Queen-mother made
" him maſter of France, and her-
" ſelf. He obtained that power over
" her,

* Mem. de Turenne.

" her, which an artful man will ac-
" quire over a woman born without
" ftrength fufficient to govern, yet
" with conftancy enough to perfift in
" her choice." All the French Hif-
torians (Vide MEZERAY, HENAULT,
&c.) agree in faying, MAZARINE's
government in a little time became fo
intolerable, that he was detefted by
the whole people, who became aftu-
ated with a factious fpirit of licentiouf-
nefs; the nobles too were difgufted,
and putting themfelves at the head of
different parties, laid the foundation of
that violent and dangerous civil war
which broke out foon afterwards.
During this conflict MAZARINE was
obliged to fly. The parliament impeached him, and fet a price upon his
head. But during his exile, he conti-
nued to govern by other hands, and
the

the influence which he retained with
the Queen-mother; who so poſſeſſed
the young King in his favour, that
his Majeſty looked upon him as a fa-
ther. Though the tranquility of the
kingdom was reſtored by the baniſh-
ment of the Cardinal, yet the court ſo
managed affairs, that the oppoſition to
him became ſo enervated, partly by its
own blunders, but chiefly by the lea-
ders liſtening to the overtures of the
Court, which the Cardinal *ſecretly* contrived to get made to them, that the
Queen-mother ſoon found ſhe might
ſafely order the King to recall him.
His Majeſty embraced him with the
moſt tender affection; and *he publicly
reſumed his power.* Even ORLEANS,
who had affected to hate him moſt,
and who thereby had gained the
eſteem of the people, was baſe enough

to

to become reconciled to him. The nobility fervilely welcomed him into the city, and the parliament, to its eternal difhonour, abjectly folicited his protection. In the midft of this more than fcandalous and infamous degeneracy, there was *one* man who remained firm againft him. This was the *Coadjutor* of ORLEANS, the great CONDE, as VOLTAIRE calls him; who had penetration enough to difco-ver many of his fecret ftratagems and treacheries, and honefty enough to refift him. But what could *one* man do. He was deferted by the party, who were fo infamous and venal as to put on the livery of the Court. And even the Parliament became fo obfequious and devoted to MAZARINE, that they condemned CONDE, becaufe he was MAZARINE's enemy. "Thus France "bubbled

" bubbled and laughed at, bent her
" neck to the defpotifm under which
" fhe languifhes to this day ; adding,
" one more proof, that the public ha-
" tred may not be the lefs followed by
" public enflavement to the perfon
" hated. *Tous les tems fe refemblent.*
All times are fimilar." And the prefent King of PRUSSIA in his examination of *Machiavel's Prince*, fays,
" that MAZARINE having furmounted
" all difficulties, deprived the Parlia-
" ment of its privileges in fuch a
" manner, that to this day it is but
" a mere phantom ; which yet fome-
" times pretends to be a real body,
" but is foon made fenfible of it's
" error."

Thefe reflections, and this part of
the French hiftory, naturally occur
to the mind of any thinking man,
who

who is at all acquainted with the tranfactions of thefe times. If we compare fimilar caufes with fimilar effects, what has not this country to fear? Will not every man fay, it was an inexcufable thing to reject that plan of adminiftration, which carried with it the obvious and convincing means of bringing *Union* and *Strength* to Government, and of rendering it formidable enough to combat, and deftroy whatever fchemes might in a few months, or perhaps weeks, be formed againft it, by the inconftancy of the man who is ever projecting fome internal mifchief?

. This is the *fecond* opportunity that has been *weakly* or *treacheroufly* loft, of gaining that afcendancy over the ficklenefs of the Favourite, which is become abfolutely neceffary to eftablifh

H   a pera permanent adminiftration. What paffed in July, laft year, is well known; and many who were not then, are, I believe, now pretty fully convinced of his power. He made the adminiftration at that time, as well as turned out their predeceffors. He has turned them out alfo, and now put in another fet. Where are thefe fluctuations to end? or what can they mean?

The nation hath long been wifhing and calling for Mr. PITT. Mr. PITT is now come, and what hath he done? I blufh for my country, which weeps over his hypocrify. He has effected his long meditated junction with the Favourite; has deferted the only place in which he could ferve his country; and, like Enoch, he is *tranf-lated* never more to be heard of.

He

He has facrificed his noble friend
and relation, and all the ties of affection, gratitude, honour, faith, and (if
he is ftill fufceptible of feeling) his
domeftic peace, to his prefent views.
How different, let him recollect, has
been the conduct of that noble Lord,
who, with a firmnefs rarely to be met
with, and with an integrity that
fpoke the zeal of his heart, fupported *him* upon many points of importance and difficulty, contrary to
the opinions of many of his beft
friends, and in danger of lofing a
very confiderable part of his prefent
poffeffions; no confideration of which
ever induced him to fwerve one moment from thofe ties of friendfhip,
and that great public caufe in which
he ftood engaged.—In January laft,
the noble Lord could have gone into

admi-

administration, if he would have taken it upon the terms that Mr. PITT, I beg pardon, now Lord CHAT-HAM, has.

There have not been wanting other opportunities, and repeated solicitations, to induce the noble Lord to accept; but he never would upon terms dishonourable to himself, and unserviceable to his country. And yet these refusals have not been dictated by either a dislike of office, or a spirit of opposition to the wishes of the people, who know his abilities, and would rejoice to see him at the head of affairs; for the business of one would be his delight, and the service of the other his pride: but by an integrity, that is now, and to latest ages will be admired, in disdaining to put on the livery of the Favourite, or

that

that of his *Vice-Roy*, the new made Peer, which is but his at fecond hand.

This truth is clealy evinced, by what has been faid was told to a Great Perfonage the fame day that the noble Lord fet out for the country; which has been fuppofed was nearly to the following effect: That the Commoner's terms were of fuch a nature, it was impoffible the noble Lord could accept of them confiftently with his honour: that his Lordfhip had made a facrifice of his Brother to the Commoner's refentment, in order to accommodate with him; but that gentleman infifted upon bringing in a fet of men, fome of whom were perfonal enemies to his Lordfhip, and with whom he had differed upon the moft effential points

of

of Government; and would not
permit him to name one friend
for the Cabinet, in whom he had
an entire confidence: and had af-
fumed a power to himfelf, to which
his Lordfhip never could fubmit;
for if he did, the world would fay,
with great juftice, that he went in like
a child, to go out like a fool. That
his wifh was, to retrieve the honour
of the Nation by an adminiftration
formed upon a broad bottom, and
compofed of men of the beft abilities,
without refpect to party, which his
firft and principal view was to extin-
guifh and annihilate, as much as poffible, in order that the whole attention
of Parliament might be confined to
the great objects of national concern.
That he had never been a fuitor to
——— either for himfelf or his
friends,

friends, for any place of honour or emolument; he did not even seek the present offer; yet he was extremely willing to sacrifice his own peace and leisure, to the service of His M. and his country, provided he could do it with honour; but that, he added, was in his own disposal, and he would make a compliment of it to no man.

In the evening (of the same day) the noble Lord told the noble lawyer who had been appointed Negotiator, that the farce was at an end, and the masque was off. His lordship need not have sent for him from the country, for there was no real wish or intention to have him in.

As no reasons were given by the Commoner for refusing the *healing* propositions of his noble Relation, the Public will very naturally, and

perhaps

perhaps very juftly, fuppofe, they were inconfiftent with the bargain he had made with the Favourite; might prove abortive of his new connection; or, which is more probable, deftructive of the Favourite's great plan of Government, which is nothing more, than to increafe the fpirit of divifion, and by perpetually playing one party againft another (having always the ———'s power in his own hands, which is a weight fufficient to throw the balance where he pleafes) he is thus able to fecure himfelf, and continue mafter of all. But had this plan of *Union* taken place, the fyftem of governing by divifion muft have been at an end; and it would not have been prudent in the Favourite to advife the difmiffion of fuch a miniftry; or refort to his old tricks of mak-

ing

ing and unmaking, only to fhew his
own power, and the fubferviency of
mankind. Such a combination of
ftrength would have been fufficient to
crufh him to atoms. He knew it;
and he feared it. Therefore by having previoufly gained the Commoner
to his intereft, he prevented the acceptance of it; and thereby effected
what he had long wifhed for, the feparation of that gentleman from his
noble relation. This feparation has,
for a confiderable time, been the dar-
ling object of his wifhes: has employed his whole thoughts; and he
has contrived an hundred ftratagems,
and meditated a thoufand ways, to accomplifh this great end. Sometimes
he has endeavoured to tempt one, and
fometimes the other, with his offers;
always taking them fingly: but the

I virtue

virtue and integrity of the noble Lord have always foiled his machinations, and, until this period, have likewife faved his relation. But a Title, and a *Side-Place* with a large falary, but no bufinefs or refponfibility annexed to it, were baits which that gentleman had long been gaping after, and which at length have caught him. Baits which his ambition could not make him more eager to fwallow, than the *Thane* was to offer. " Wonder not therefore " that he has changed fides and opi- " nions; that he has united with him " whom he pretended to hate; fince " all fides, and all opinions, which " promote his views, are equally eligi- " ble to him." But it will be matter of wonder indeed, if this new friend- fhip lafts. It is too great a victory to the Favourite, too great a triumph to the

court, not to be followed with a total defeat. He will be turned out, as he
hath been turned in ; only to add, if
poffible, fomething more to that public odium and abhorrence of his name
and character, which have fo unani-
moufly followed his apoftacy and
promotion; his defertion of his
friends and his country, and the ac-
complifhment of his long fought
wretched alliance with the Favourite; who now laughs at his folly,
defpifes his vanity, exults over his
weaknefs, and rejoices in the Public
execration of fuch an Hypocrite. In
a word, it is the *perfection* of the Favourite's fcheme ; which no refiftance,
no integrity, no virtue of the noble
Lord could prevent ; met, as it was,
more than half way, by the luft of

Power, *Honours*, and employment, the ingratitude and perfidy of —— ——.

With whom, befides, is the late Commoner in league? with thofe very men who he hated moft and de-fpifed: with General CONWAY, who two years ago he refufed to fee at Hayes, though preffed to it in the ftrongeft manner by Lord LYTTEL-TON; with Lord SHELBURNE, upon whom he put a negative laft year, when nominated to the very office he now enjoys; with Colonel BARRE, who called him an heap of contradic-tions, &c. &c.

If it is afked, why had he fo great a *Penchant* for them now? The anfwer is, becaufe the firft, in a great meafure, laid the foundation of the furrender of the Honour and Authority of Great Britain, and made a tender of both

at

at the feet of the Colonies; the second affifted him, and the third follows of courfe.

This little corps, contemptible in numbers, and defpicable in abilities, is to be reinforced by the fubalterns of the late miniftry; by thofe whofe exceffive luft for office, whofe ingratitude, meannefs, and fubferviency, would not fuffer them to follow the *refignations* and *difmiffions* of their patrons. The moment thefe heard there was another recruiting ferjeant in town; they inftantly deferted both the officers and colours under which they had firft enlifted, and for prefent pay, and good quarters, repaired to the drum head of the enemy.——*Video omnes damnatos omnefque ignominiâ affectos, illàc facere.* Cic.

To

To the Gentlemen *out*, I beg leave
to fay a few words. You are now the
only men from whom the Public hope
for that fecurity of their moft valua-
ble interefts which they had long been
taught to expect from others, who
have now betrayed them. And being
poffeffed of great and real property in
the kingdom, you are moft naturally
and nearly interefted in the public
welfare, and may truly be ftiled, the
conftitutional reprefentatives and guar-
dians of the people. It fhould be
therefore, and I make no doubt it is,
with you, matter of confideration, whether the moft effential points of public
bufinefs, the reftoration of *union* and
tranquility to the nation, the honour
of the crown abroad, and the authority of government at home, can be
properly executed, attained and fecur-
ed

ed by any but an able, powerful and public spirited administration ? Whether rescuing your country out of the hands of a *Faction*, formed by an unnatural connection between the Deserter of the people and the Favourite of the Court; and from the designs of a dangerous conspiracy against the public peace; be not objects worthy your most serious attention; and the first steps, now become indispensible, towards forming an administration adequate to the difficulties and necessities of the times? In this great, this truly patriotic work, there is no doubt but you will have the assistance and support of all good men, all real well-wishers to their country. *Libertas et anima nostra in dubio est.* Sall.

Such

Such is a fhort and plain enquiry into fome parts of the extraordinary conduct of a late Right Honourable Commoner. Very few obfervations are neceffary to affift any reader in forming a right judgment upon them; therefore as few as poffible have been introduced. The facts will fpeak for themfelves, and leave that impreffion and conviction behind them, which are ever the companions of truth. But to thofe few, thofe very few, who have yet the hardinefs to appear in his defence, and becaufe they can fay nothing better, are obliged to fay only this, *Let us wait, let us fee his Meafures*; —I will make a fhort remark. The Public did wait until they faw his meafures; they were filent. But when the noble Lord, his relation, re-turned into the country, they feared

all

all was not well. In a few days his
meafures appeared : and they are ; a
junction with the Favourite, to which
he has facrificed his old connections,
and beft friends ; and the acquifition
of a Title, to which, as far as he was
able, he has facrificed the Public.

I cannot conclude without the
warmeft thanks, I think I may fay
in the name of every Englifhman, to
the fteady difcerning, and patriotic
Members of the Common Council of
the City of London ; who when repeated attempts were made to furprife
them into an addrefs, upon an appoint-
ment of men, and an adoption of
meafures, equally obnoxious and inju-
rious to the nation, *refufed*, with a
firmnefs that does the greateft honour
to their public fpirit ; and told the
perfon applying, " *That the Commoner*

K

*was caught in a fcotch trap, and he muft
get out as well as he could.*"—To fruftrate
the efforts of a DINGLEY*, may there
never be wanting the good fenfe and
fpirit of a FREEMAN†.—They difdained to fet an example of deceit to
the Public, and fpurned, with a laud-
able indignation, the fcandalous attempts upon their underftandings and
integrity, to become the inftruments
of impofition upon their fellow fub-
jects; to ferve the bafe, felf-interefted
purpofes of a contemptible *Faction*,
and cover the moft abandoned and infamous apoftacy.

MOURN, ALBION mourn, the wretched chance
   deplore;
In CHATHAM buried, WILLIAM PITT's no more!

   B——, thou arch-foe to Freedom and her Friends,
At length thy fubtile craft has gain'd its ends.
Divide and *govern* is thy maxim ftill ;
Lo! *Difcord* flies, fubfervient to thy will,
                       Whirling

   * Mr. Charles Dingley.
   † Mr. Samuel Freeman.

Whirling her brand of blue, fulphurious flame,
And PITT and TEMPLE, are no more the fame.

   O PITT, thou Prince of Patriots! ah! how
     chang'd!
Now with a STUART, by a STUART, rang'd;
'Scap'd from the wiles of a quinquennial fnare,
But caught at laft, altho, the hook was bare;
BUTE hands thee in, MACKENZIE at thy fide,
Difplays *his* Private feal, with Publick Pride.

   Triply exalted, penfion'd, titled, plac'd,
Thy heart yet whifpers, " PITT, thou art abas'd!
" PYNSENT hath murder'd Faith, all Faith is o'er
" With CHATHAM therefore; PITT finds faith
     no more!"

   Think how, purfuing Freedom's fteady plan,
And call'd by BUTE, th' *impracticable man*;
Mafter of all that virtue e'er defir'd,
Thy Country lov'd thee, and her foes admir'd!
Then think how, (triumph plum'd upon his brow)
He boafts to have found thee *practicable* now!

   Erewhile thy Country's pride, fupport, and joy,
Thou'rt loft thine honour, and haft gain'd a toy!
Can the vain title folid blifs afford?
Do thine ears tingle at the name of LORD?
Reflect how much thy glory fhone more clear,
In *Stephen s Chapel*; there thou hadft no PEER!
Shall not the weight of TEMPLE bear thee down,
While confcious firmnefs animates his frown?
Shall not *unverfar'd* LYTTELTON purfue,
Unclogg'd by *one*, th' incumber'd flave of *two*?

                 O fhame

O fhame to patriotifm ! her name is grown
A Butt for laughter; PYNSENT's *Price* is known !—
Yet ftill remain fome honeft hearts, and hands,
To raife her ftandard—TEMPLE ! lead the bands !
Till on the FAVOURITE's ftubborn neck thou tread,
And crufh to atoms his detefted Head !

N. C. M. S. C.

F I N I S.

BOOKS Printed for J. ALMON, oppofite Bur-
lington-Houfe, Piccadilly.

I. THE HISTORY of the MINORITY, during the Years 1762, 1763, 1764 and 1765.
Exhibiting the CONDUCT, PRINCIPLES, and VIEWS
of that PARTY. The FOURTH EDITION, with
ADDITIONS. Price 5 s. bound, or 4 s. fewed.

☞ *The* very extraordinary, *and almoft* fingular
Succefs *which this Book hath already met with, is the
ftrongeft and beft Teftimony of its* Merit. *It has more-
over been tranflated in Holland, France, and other Na-
tions ; in which, as well as in England, it is* much read
and efteemed.

II. The PRINCIPLES of the CHANGES in 1765 impar-
tially examined. The Fourth Edition. Price 1s. 6d.

III. Two PROTESTS againft the Repeal of the American Stamp Act, together with Lifts of the *Minority*
upon that Queftion, in both Houfes of Parliament.
Price only 1s.

IV. A COLLECTION of the moft INTERESTING
TRACTS which were lately Publifhed in England
and America, on the Subjects of TAXING the AME-
RICAN COLONIES, and REGULATING their
TRADE. In two Volumes, Price 14 s. bound.

V. A COLLECTION of the moft ESTEEMED POLITI-
CAL TRACTS which appeared during the Years 1763,
1764, and 1765. In four Volumes. Price 1 s. 4 d.
bound.

www.ingramcontent.com/pod-product-compliance
Lightning Source LLC
Chambersburg PA
CBHW020253290326
41930CB00039B/1207